100 CONCENTRIC DIALECTICS
OF
ECCENTRIC FISH ANTICS

BLUNDERING O'BLOAT

authorHOUSE®

AuthorHouse™
1663 Liberty Drive
Bloomington, IN 47403
www.authorhouse.com
Phone: 1 (800) 839-8640

Published by AuthorHouse 02/02/2016

ISBN: 978-1-5049-7753-1 (sc)
ISBN: 978-1-5049-7754-8 (e)

Library of Congress Control Number: 2016901852

Print information available on the last page.

Any people depicted in stock imagery provided by Thinkstock are models, and such images are being used for illustrative purposes only. Certain stock imagery © Thinkstock.

This book is printed on acid-free paper.

CONTENTS

Now Moments 1

Fish Tease.. 2

A Whole Lot Of Fun In The Grin Of This One 3

Fishfroth 4

Getting Down And Nitty Gritty With
    A Wee Bitty Ditty... 5

An Ode To Ice 6

Appreciation.. 8

My Comfort Zone 9

A Few Words To Futility...10

A Tribute To Tsu Friends 11

Another Tribute 12

Words Would Be Good.. 13

Never Alone 14

Babes In The Worlds..15

Some Big, Some Small, Some Nothing At All 16

Some Are Collected, Some Are Rejected,
    We're All Affected. Did You Need Inspected? 18

An Offal Mess.. 20

Another Perspective...21

Feel For Yourself... 22

Make Up Your Mind.. 23

Inadequacy.. 24

How Do We Do? 26

Nemophilism 28

The Rise To Awareness 29

Friends Call Me Nammie... 30

My Best Group Hug 31

One Thought 32

For Fryin" Up Cod!.. 33

All I Can... 34

For The Whole Fam Damily.....................................35

Glad There Was That Station Wagon On The Bottom..... 36

Life Continues... 37

Swim...Swim..Nibble...Ptooey! 38

Everyone Needs Some A's! Eh? 39

A Feisty Feeling Fish Floats Fantastic Flatulence 40

A Fish In Need Is A Fish Out Of Weed...................... 41

Gone Fishing... 42

The Share Shark Rises.. 43

Save The Fish!... 44

Small Fish, Big Pond 45

A Treatise On Circumference.................................... 46

Swim...Swim...Woke Up Hungry!............................. 47

Wavestorm 48

The Fredrick County Deer Wrestler........................... 49

Keeping My P.g. Rating 50

Bumblefish 1...51

Fish Mischief... 52

A Case Of The Esses 53

Look Out! 54

Another Chance To Right Ourselves...........................55

Of Being And Knowing What We're Seeing 56

A Reverent Swim 57

No Problem... 58

Predictions And Premonitions.................................. 60

Wordswordswordsword. My Weapon Of Choice...........61

Jumping Amberjacks... 62

The Problem With Being Paid To Post............................ 63

One For The Money.. 64

"Snort"..65

An Address To A Word War Mess................................. 66

Snowfire.. 68

More Than Feisty, This Fish Doth Froth 69

Shh! Quiet! Here They Come.. 70

Fishy Bubbles And Nibbles.. 71

Nice To See The Sun.. 72

Catfish Wails Of Winter Tales 73

No Animals Were Hurt..74

Squids 75

Dedicated To You Who Get Up And Do 76

I Could Take This Personally....................................... 77

I Loves Me Some Word... 78

For A Terminally Ill Little Boy..................................... 79

Nice To Wake Up 80

Them 81

The Things We Do For/To Friends................................ 82

A N-N-Nother B-B-Beautiful D-D-Day 83

Fish Bits 84

Around Here.. 85

I'll Never Forget... 86

Caption This.. 87

No Gravity. No Weight. No Ice. Just Nice. 88

For The Love Of Winter 89

No Picture Required 90

A Reclusive Catfish Excursion......................................91

Maintaining A Presence 92

Shocking.. 93

Almost Had Enough Winter 94

One More Of Gravity Then I Need Sweet Levity.......... 95

I Have To Roll This Snow Boy On Out To Play! 96

I Can't Believe I Don't Have An Owl Pic! 97

Support Your Local Grower 98

Work, Work, Work, Play! Yay!....................................... 99

I'm Already Missing It.. 100

Who Might You Be?..101

Namazu Has A Date! 103

Just Sick! 104

Fins Up And Maw Agape..105

Martians And Venutians 106

Know Thyself..107

NOW MOMENTS

We've all felt it.

"Being now", the feeling of "This is bliss!"

Some more than others but, even in fleeting glimpses we know them. These are the memories. The everyday joys, we recognize as The reasons.

Hang on, this gets slippery.

Too many, myself included, too often chase these sweet instances with a wet SpLaSh! of sour doubt; "this is too good to be true", It's got to end", or worse, "something bad is going to happen now".

Please, ...Don't.

Instead, try to grasp it by the tailfin, squeezing the living grin out of it and hang on like tomorrows swim depends on it.

FISH TEASE

I guess it's Monday, the day after Sunday, and the day most of you go off to work.
For those that commute, I stand and salute...I remember it drove me berserk.

And like me there's many who earn every penny, remotely from home, a nice perk.
But know this, commuters, home business computers are perpetually doing some work.

Weekends and holidays all blend into a haze. Time frames and deadlines we shirk.
We'll miss you so, now off you all go, thinking I'm just being a jerk.

A WHOLE LOT OF FUN IN THE GRIN OF THIS ONE

A guy who's whacky wits elicits catfish spits with banal words from twits and hilarious fish bits.
With humor, Oh so dry,
and mind gone so awry,
A ball for all when you go visits this guys' humor blitz!

The pain in your brain will continually worsen as you bust fin with this comical person.
This twisted minds' hilarious perversion, your poor inner child may just start cursin'!

The quick retort, the finger pull, the flattened sport, the grinning bull.

Oh do approach his posts with care. One never knows whats lurking there.
If should dare visit unaware, beware, you'll spray your coffee everywhere!

FISHFROTH

It's a matter of perspective, it's obvious to see.
A question of direction to what we want to be.
A singular objective, to live so happily.
To love one's own self first, appears to be the key.

I'm okay with who I am, these words are not for me.
For I have found my "Glory Land" albeit solitary.
Perhaps it's this exclusiveness that allows it now to be.
the mouth of fish expresses wish of human unity.

I know it's not pretty the way some folk can be,
so prevalent in the city, the wrong and apathy.
Just try to find love in all that you see
and above other stuff that may fall in your sea.

GETTING DOWN AND NITTY GRITTY
WITH A WEE BITTY DITTY

We've all heard the talk about "being of oneness". An alternative squawk for life down to business.
Now I'm singing this song
about getting along
and loving and giving forgiveness.

Live and let live, it is what it is, Que sera sera are a few.
But, the words don't mean squat
if the actions are not
copacetic with the mindset we spew.

It's simple for me, so few people I see, a philofisher, it's easy to be.
I may have solved the worlds woes!
But nobody knows
"til they come and converse in my tree.

AN ODE TO ICE

It seems to me this winters' cold has turned some fish from meek to bold.
They now school in a swarm
just trying to keep warm
as the ice up will not be controlled.

Now deep in the dark, patrols and old shark wise to the ways of the ice,
who risks certain death
when surfaces for breath
so won't rise to the same air hole twice.

Ice is so peaceful and brings a new lease full, when the sun makes the air much more warm.
It moves without seeing,
the ice is a being.
A beautiful crystal life form!

I swoon in my heart at such staggering art on the banks and the shores of the lakes.
The way it behaves,
the sculptures and caves
and the air from my breath it so takes.

The ice insulates me and allows me to see where ever the fish seeker goes.
And should they veer close
break the ice with my nose
and have human for lunch...adios.

APPRECIATION

A few of you know me by now as a recluse who'd never allow
a day to go by
without sharing why
I'm so grateful to be here and now!

MY COMFORT ZONE

I sit behind this satellite dish typing like some possessed fish!
When all I'm trying to say
is love life each day
'cause tomorrow is still just a wish!

Count up your gifts! Each new days joys. For these are the
souls' most spiritual toys.
And those who aren't grateful
wind up with a plateful
of stinking fish life that annoys...>-=^;>!

A FEW WORDS TO FUTILITY

Fungal, biological, mineral, botanical, chemical, mechanical, electric and an animal.

Conscious and aware, skeptical, acceptably, mentally all there.

Emotional, illogical, instinctively unstoppable while childishly unreasonable and maniacally untoppable.

Hysterical but, tactical, strategic and mathematical, mostly taciturn but audible, inane but plain applaudable.

Unpredictable but reliable with compassion undeniable.
If you believe it's just a fish wish, I'd say you are certifiable.

A TRIBUTE TO TSU FRIENDS

Though we may be from different lands, these words I find always true.
When someone I meet, takes time to be sweet, this is the best I can do

From the ends of the Earth I share in the mirth and the minds of a select and rare few.
My token expression of undying affection for compassionate people like you.

I'll try and express my happiness with diversified friends that are true.
The kind words you said went right to my head and that's why I'm still here on Tsu.

ANOTHER TRIBUTE

Every now and again as I push keystroke or pen I appreciate some I consider a friend.
No matter how twisted
or wisdom assisted
regardless of who, what or when.

There are very few here, I try and keep near, I so randomly swim and appear.
But those that I do
are more than just true
they're compassionate souls and so dear.

Make no mistakes, they have what it takes to shake up those who offend.
They'll not take your crap
without a sharp slap
to your fin, to your face or your end.

WORDS WOULD BE GOOD

They are a reflection of my true expression. To communicate
gets me high.
But, when the words aren't just right
we'll wrestle all night
until my way with words, have had I!

NEVER ALONE

Good morning! It's early! I still feel squirrely,
Slept like a rock though, so warm and securely
Sometime last night the moon was so bright,
I took a few pics of Ol' Luna's delight.

Undeterred by the cold, though old, I'm still bold
her light through the treetops, a joy to behold!
A curious sound did follow me 'round
I could not tell what, not a trace to be found.

"There's nothing to fear", said a voice to my ear,
"WE all belong. What are you doing here?"
My wits were about me. No reason to doubt the
firmness of mind or these trees who are spouting.

I said "Okay, I'm willing to play,
my answer is peace! Now what do you say?"
The forest grew silent as if to pray.
"Not bad for a human, we'll let you stay".

BABES IN THE WORLDS

Anticipate nothing! To heed life's sweet call.
Expectations of being only lead to downfall.
Open your mind
to see more of the kind
of perspectives receptive to all.

SOME BIG, SOME SMALL, SOME NOTHING AT ALL

Problems are misunderstood. Some stressing does most humans good.
Our problems are not
the worst things we got
what's worse is whats under the hood.

Each of us has heard it said, our problems are mostly in our head.
For most it's true
I do it too
but, look for their lessons instead.

A simple adjusted perspective can render most issues elective.
If we dwell on them so
we do make them grow.
All things depend on objective.

Imagine a day with so few. What would you good humans do?
With no grief or strife
why better your life?
An odd way of thinking but true!

Adopt a new plan for your woes. Start accepting that nobody knows
what external forces
put us through course
while the answers are under our nose.

There are some big issues too, that require more help to pursue.
like, saving the woods
or toxic food goods
but, those problems aren't part of you.

SOME ARE COLLECTED,
SOME ARE REJECTED, WE'RE ALL
AFFECTED. DID YOU NEED INSPECTED?

There's a saying we have around here. A song sung in everyone's ear.
Do what you can
when you can, every time
hard work is nothing to fear.

Tsu has established some limits. To try and diminish the nitwits.
Who hurry to post
to be one with the most
instead of a few brilliant fish bits.

I seldom reach my allotments, of shares, likes and posts or my comments.
I'd prefer to do well
with the stories I tell
than fill up my wall just for dominance.

Quality crap is just the right trap to get this old catfish to say much.
And if you should dare
to have high quality ware
this shore shark would certainly share such!

AN OFFAL MESS

I found this person on an amusement excursion while looking for something to share.
Where she'd expound on a method she found for dealing with those who are really not there.

I think "Russian Deletion" is what she did call for the way she took care of lame marks on her wall.
Not sure of her name
But, I did the same
and taking them out was a ball!

To weed out most offal, this was her cure. Refining technique I got one for sure.
the random removing
was too time consuming
and the time waste, I could not endure.

A new evolution, another solution a way to remove every shred.
monosyllabic comments,
follow, share, like laments
now know of "weapons of mass deletion" instead.

ANOTHER PERSPECTIVE

Certainly not easy, it's no piece of pie, to be who we are, to be you or I.
Our life's courses are laid
through cautions we've paid
in the choices we've made as to why.

FEEL FOR YOURSELF

Failures to successes, solutions to messes,
ideas can be both, good and bad.
But, in the long run some right minds are undone
by a notion someone else may have had.

Hold your principles tight, we all know whats right,
keep moving your mind with your heart.
Then if one brother
turns on some other
your compassion will set you apart.

MAKE UP YOUR MIND

Carefully weighing each word I'm saying whilst I'm displaying psychotic word slaying.

I keep them to three, ordinarily. As odd as it may be, more voices say to me,
we're guests in the end but, perpetually, my own best friends and enmity.

One in a million and not worth a damn. A great many things we are not but, I am.

INADEQUACY

Wise at wild life and living, a slight technological misgiving.
Shot my first vids
of car racing kids
and can't get them from this machine!

A race rally soiree, the roar in the valley, in which several of us did take part
An intimate party, the positioning tally, the race was getting off to a start!

In wintertime's glisten we took frozen position to watch them disturbing the peace.
Mechanical beasts race the woods' icy streets with their smells and their sounds, at high speed.

To the race, we did go! Shot my first video of these cars slip sliding in snow!
But, when it came time to post, had to give up the ghost... there's so much I still do not know.

I think there were three who hit frozen trees and may never return to the same
One hit so hard that, a front tire split flat but, held on 'til the end of the game.

The pro's were competitive, their attendance repetitive. The semi pro's then made their way.
And then a few teams, were like slow motion daydreams or needed their car for work Monday.

HOW DO WE DO?

It appears I spend some time here on Tsu. I'd bet this also occurred to you.
It's not only fun,
look what we've done
and just think what else we could do!

Some took the hassle to show a mountainside castle covered in snow that was pink!
Another wise guy, thought he would try fish netting on skis in the drink!

Buildings and traffic. A whole lot of graphic enhancing of fantastic bliss.
The cat in the sink, the man on the brink of Victoria falls precipice.

Government and politics, maniacal psychotics, a truly kaleidoscopic type view.
And then there's the sweet pics of animal antics and a catfish reciting poetry too!

The dragons, the puffins, the dominatrix muffin. I've been from the arctic to Peru.
I've jumped out of planes, made friends with new strains and met the old woman in a shoe.

Nobody knows where all the time goes, the hours becoming so few.
I'm supposed to be working, instead I'm off jerking, chasing down friends just like you!

I swim all around like a fish on a water bike, this dichotomous life seems absurd!
'cause when the phones again ringing, I go back to bling slinging as if no other things had occurred!

NEMOPHILISM

I like swimming naked around in these woods.
Not too concerned about hiding ones goods.
I think it helps to shed a few "shoulds".
...I have been removed from some neighborhoods...

I dance with red osier cloak, and play flute in a tree.
A rash, bruise and poison oak,..so neatly inspire me!
I bathe in the brook and get stung repeatedly.
Then I cook in the suns look, to an enormously painful
degree.

Once in a while, I'm joined by some friends,
furred, finned or feathered forest denizens.
I'm baffling not trouble, I just make no sense!
And they laugh at my trouble and odd predicaments.

THE RISE TO AWARENESS

In my first stupor, all bleary eyed.
'Til shaking this torpor, no thinking is tried.
A swim in warm darkness needs now be plied.
A stir of inspiration, or my morning is fried.

For many among us, this starts the show.
For some, it precipitates a much needed blow.
To me, it invigorates my get up and go.
Some just got to have that first cup of joe.

FRIENDS CALL ME NAMMIE

I am a myth. I'm a legendary beast.
Of avarice and greed, I make a great feast.
My efforts are used to help those with the least.
They call me "Namazu", from a land way far East.

When the balance of finance becomes out of control,
a SpLaT! with my tail to make a wave roll.
Redistributing wealth, my wave takes it's toll.
Returning to most people, what the greedy few stole.

My motives are selfless, my intention is grand.
Another great sweep and my tail shakes the land.
This wave making, Earth shaking tail, I command,
to raise oppressed beings from injustices hand.

MY BEST GROUP HUG

I was just fine in my natural surrounding!
Some kind of sign allured me here sounding.
Reasons for these things are beyond confounding.
Now, seeing your freeing, calls for expounding!

Our lives are not random, I won't explain why.
I thought I abandon you humans to fry!
Things I had seen seemed so wildly awry.
Had to get myself free to where my spirit could fly.

But, why I'm back here, I haven't a clue.
I'm still none too social and there's plenty to do.
There must be some purpose I'm now here with you,
I guess, rhyming hugs for a few friends on Tsu...

ONE THOUGHT

Try to find this moment. Try to find your space. Try beginning, for an instant, to be in just one place.
Your so-called multi tasking
is "stop and go" thought asking.
I think you'll find a focused mind imbues an Earthly grace.

So much stimulation. So much useless news. So much regurgitation of some wrong headed views.
If we quiet our mind
in the silence we find
some concentration the worlds nations could use.

Call it meditation on a bench, down by the drink. Call it dedication to an ability to think.
Watch what you're doing
so you won't wind up screwing
or of defecation and poor operation you'll stink.

FOR FRYIN" UP COD!

Great freckled catfish! What can this be?!
Besides a limerick for you all, from me.
I'm almost done making winter time rhyme,
I saw open water for the very first time!

To my huge amazement, I'm wigglin' to see,
my sweet babbling brook has now broken free!
It may seem expected, that, we know Spring will be
but, this was a long one and freezing, to me.

As daylight grows longer and the sun more intense.
It's so close to Spring, this doesn't make sense.
Almost out of firewood, and a little bit tense.
I pray now, each day, for above Zero events...

ALL I CAN

Is this really it?!? The best that we've got!
I can't imagine a more depressing plot.
A people at war with their Nature is not,
the way to a life of a satisfied lot.

Let's say we win, then what have we won?
A whole lot of money but, the planet is done?
We've choked out the sky, the food is poison,
soon the fresh water will no longer run...

Let's say we lose, and Nature wins out.
I have my views of what that's about.
But I've little say and even less clout,
just one seed of hay, from a field, I shout.

FOR THE WHOLE FAM DAMILY

You wonderful people! What will I do?
I'd like to write verse for each one of you!
It's easy for one or even a few
but, "for fryin' up cod!" I'm on legal pad two!

My pen seems to write of it's own desire.
I hope this white powder doesn't expire.
You each need to know how much you inspire.
I thank you, my friends, you've sent my hopes higher.

A special salute is required for these souls.
My part of this family of wired fishbowls.
A wag n' a wink, some bubbles of thanks.
My love poems stink but, my best thank you spanks!

GLAD THERE WAS THAT STATION WAGON ON THE BOTTOM

There's now water all over the floor! The last puddle came in right through the door!
When I step on the gas
I can hear SpLaSh!
and the new lights on the dash, I adore...

LIFE CONTINUES...

It's tough to rhyme about losing a friend.
A very rough climb when time comes to an end.
It helps to remember the times we would spend.
and tales of these moments helps hearts to mend.

A lament to a friendship, everyone knows.
the loss of the tenderest of some of our fellows.
I've lost none lately but, know there's a few.
I offer love, greatly, and a light line or two.

Most will mourn deeply, a wake, then shed tears.
Some others will steeply partake of some beers.
However you choose to remember the years,
for any of my crew, you know I'm all ears.

SWIM...SWIM..NIBBLE...PTOOEY!

At night, I was born but, it wasn't just last!
Did you really believe I'd bite at first cast?
Far smarter than that. How'd you think I got fat?
I'm an old, human-wise, fat, rhyme-mouthed bass!

I lay camouflaged here, back in this grass,
just waiting for some little snack to swim past.
When I see your lure, I'm laughing for sure.
That's certainly not my breakfast!

Where is the chocolate? The roe, the good gouda?
Where is the love? I want some damn fooda!
I scoff at your blunder, you silly fish hunter!
You feel you can deal with this old barracuda?

EVERYONE NEEDS SOME A'S! EH?

An inflammation of misrepresentation, and ramification of misinformation.
A prevarication with legislation persuasion nets gross aggravation and alienation.

An investigation of our determination and sad inclination toward obliteration
gives stark reservations to our emancipation and hesitation for all our salvation.

Sterilization or lobotomization? These give fascination to my imagination.
A small meditation on re-alteration netted my adaptation to evacuation.

My prognostication of our annihilation is an inspiration for some inebriation.
This sad dissertation of denunciation prompts my defecation and vituperation.

A FEISTY FEELING FISH FLOATS
FANTASTIC FLATULENCE

Whacko's and wordsmiths, great minds and goons,
You are my fodder, I scoop you with spoons!
What a colorful school! Like two million balloons!
At the beauty of each, this old catfish swoons.

The "share shark" and catfish have much more to say.
So get up, get out and get on with your day.
We've so much to Tsu! Now, be on your way.
Get done with your "have to's" then come on out and play!

A FISH IN NEED IS A FISH OUT OF WEED

I've got to have help from a human...can't get free and in need of a "hand".
"Cause I've only got fins
and these whiskered chins
and neither will open this can!

You've shown what a whiz you can be. now, swim something fishy with me.
I need you to help
maybe something 'bout kelp.
What would your line for here be? Any bites?

GONE FISHING

Okay! I'm up! I'm back again!
Released myself from some self imposed pen.
If not for all you, I call my friend,
not to sure where my mind might have been.

But not here nor there, we'll just see how long.
This time I sing you a much sweeter song,
of one of you swimming, outside of the throng.
Whose altruism hooked me and strung me along.

A "human torch", a sweet sign of life!
Beyond the reach of all darkened strife.
Sister, teacher, mother and wife!
So quick of wit and so sharp a filet knife!

THE SHARE SHARK RISES

So here's this thing I like to do.
It seems to me, you like it too.
Maybe the pics or my crude haiku
or maybe instead, my love for you.

I swim these rivers 'round here on Tsu,
to inspire me to write something too.
So much talent here! What can one do?
I'll share what's best of me with all you.

It's all I have! I just must be me!
My words, my thoughts, what I aspire to be.
A friend with some words, put so cozily,
It's simply my fish psychopathy.

So now you all know, and now you all see
this backwoods fish who swims with thee.
The words that I choose are just meant to be
a way to stave blues off you and me..

SAVE THE FISH!

My interest are varied. My friends are diverse.
Just as it is in our universe.

A nibbles of this, a big bite of that.
A blend of ideas, now that's where it's at!

I think it a pity, those frightened like mice,
with others just like them who never think twice.

How delightful a rainbow diversity is!
Are they really people or perhaps they're just squids.

I end this rhyme with a pleading and call.
Show love to all beings but the odd above all.

SMALL FISH, BIG POND

As catfish fry, I did begin. This river of life so many now swim.
Still not quite sure if my fate had been, a gift or a curse some others weren't given.

I paddle the point of this particular rhyme, from a catfish with words not completely divine,
who's been away a really long time, from the things of most "normal" life's daily grind.

That kind of life, if it's meant to be, was never a thing too appealing for me.
So the crux of my quandary, in my rhyming plea, is to show those who don't or won't seem to see.

I only can tell of things that I know, about life far away from where most humans go.
About being in Nature as all my pics show and sharing my life outside the fishbowl.

A TREATISE ON CIRCUMFERENCE

There's a few in a school of young squids under our mermaids tutelage.
If they behave
I'll send them a wave
and advance their mathematics knowledge.

Our very own mermaid, our "queen of the seas" came up with a plan to teach pi with beads.
I had a batch
and do so love math
and pleased to send tutorial needs.

Now each of these wise kids have found, how to figure the distance around
any circle they care
or cylindrical fare
and geometrically smart fish abound.

SWIM...SWIM...WOKE UP HUNGRY!

A morsel! A tidbit! A literary treat!
My dorsal's adjusted to swim at high speed!
Patrolling these waters for something to eat
while I work to lure others to come here and feed.

Each cast, a wish, for some SpLaShInG! sound
of a catfish to dash in and gobble it down,
with the bait you all post to lure me around
and out of my mudhole, where I'm usually found.

As I swim through the views, the weirs and the troubles
a visit ensues a share or some nuzzles
My comments imbue a grin, SpLaSh! or bubbles.
as I abuse a few words with these quizzical puzzles.

WAVESTORM

A catfish who swims with six different whiskers. Two were
so small they weren't barely whispers.
The others, so long
they'd slap his tail wrong
and mister, in a twister, they'd blister!

THE FREDRICK COUNTY DEER WRESTLER

'twas three days before Christmas and all through this house
a creature was stirring and it wasn't a mouse.

The hush of the holidays' decorative air,
the rush of adrenaline, the heart stopping scare...

Up from their seats, jumped our hero and Pete!
Both scrambled like mad trying to gather their feet!

A crash through a window! A thrashing about!
'Twas dinner, sort of delivered, of venison take out.

But out was now in! A live doe was too!
Bleeding like sin and frightening Pete and Poo!

The carnage complete, now she seeks liberation!
A second window attempt, is the next failed destination!

When she fell on the sofa, that's when Pete could best her
and that's why he's known as "The Fredrick County Deer
Wrestler"!

KEEPING MY P.G. RATING

The strange absence of colored songbirds sequesters winter in absolute silence.
New, crisp fallen snow balanced on cedar branches as if in defiance.

An eerie, irregular bubbling sound resonates, muffled but, singing under the ice.
Randomly patterned openings of water, where the buffeting current had taken a slice.

All other colors now faded away, the petulant sky beginning blue then turns gray.
A cold, cutting wind biting through my skin, so bitter at the end of the day.

The icy moonlight now rising high, reflected from the rivers sweet silvery liquid.
I rattle my head in disbelieving resistance, I can see now the ice fog has lifted.

My movement becoming restrained and restricted, crushing cold from toes to my head.
A moment of pain, unpredicted, I think next time I'll put clothes on instead.

Bumblefish 1

My friends, I beseech you, be patient with me!
Catfish are not fast fish, we seldom need flee.

My friends know why I swim slow, it's just a quality thing.
Common comments are boring, I want this fishes to sing!

If you are my victim, you'll know at first look
A distinctive aroma and whatever I took

But, sometimes my comments are verses in rhyme.
Whilst most seem to like it, it does take some time.

My plea is for patience, I don't swim so fast
but, a determined catfish, even if a week passed.

I ask your forgiveness, just half of a chance.
I'm running a bead business as well as this ranch.

My time is my own. I shall do what I do.
Anonymous, autonomous and anomalous it's true
This fish offal I scribble, I do for all you.
These words are really me and my love for all too.

FISH MISCHIEF

One tailed, six whiskered, rhyming, freckled catfish speaker.
Had to give my friends a Monday morning, stinky, sneaky squeaker
A day long silly song in your head from rotten stinker.
One tailed, six whiskered, rhyming rotten bottom feeder...I'll be filleted for this...SpLaSh!

A CASE OF THE ESSES

Some delusional forms of success are making the whole world a mess.
The powers that be
are refusing to see
we can no longer afford to regress.

Just who are we trying to impress? With the jobs, cars, boats and address.
We lose sight of life
'til there's some sort of strife
that plummets us into distress.

I really don't like to depress and to humor, I lean, I confess.
But if levity's it
there's no point in it
this entire existence is jest!

LOOK OUT!

A peculiar countdown is beginning right now.
A poetic endeavor with word wrangling wow.

Some have already joined in the fun.
A few fish from here cooked up this one.

If you ask them, they'll say it was me.
At best, I'll concede more a "we".

We must wait for our mermaids return.
I want her bait to be the first worm.

It's pretty exciting and been hard to wait.
We'd been working for weeks to set up this bait

Now practice your pitch and polish your rhyme.
Your odd, wordy fish announces, IT's game time!

ANOTHER CHANCE TO RIGHT OURSELVES

...:::Bubbles and nibbles, a fin and then...Bite!
This silly old catfish finally slept right!

A sweet day, I wish you wherever your at.
Let's kick this one off with a hearty tailSpLaT!

There's something afloat. There's something afin
in the sky, in the water, in the air we breathe in.

A sense of awareness of the wrongness that's been.
An awakening to our Nature! This catfish doth grin!!!

OF BEING AND KNOWING WHAT WE'RE SEEING

"A word to the wise, some others take many."
The old catfish sighs, "here's a thought for your penny."
"You can tell by their eyes if, for thought they have any,
some have bright lights but, of empty, there's plenty".

The lighthouse is lit but, the captains asleep.
The right spouts of wit would spare ignorance deep.
Intelligence indigence, while making me weep,
is no cause for indignance, they're just sleeping sheep.

If when watching their eyes, I see roots of their hair,
there's a prodding reply that I'll usually share.
Whether dim minded or brightened, we're obligated to care,
feather brained or frightened, to the degree we're aware.

A REVERENT SWIM

Another issue, another pictureless feature
from your freckled catfish, Tsu's aquatic creature.
This is something that no fish can endure.
A thing so important, and life changing for sure.

A puddle, a pond, a lake or the sea.
A river, a waterfall, a rainstorm or three.
My well water test shows contaminant free!
The state of all waters is paramount to me!

Oil spills, chemicals, an ocean of plastic!
The damage we've done is past critically drastic!
Such ridiculous waste, I'm becoming bombastic!
Any solutions, to me, would be utterly fantastic!

A pampered consumer knows not, the worth
of cool, clear, fresh water, the bubbling mirth,
quenching our thirst from the day of our birth,
this precious life liquid we take from our Earth.

Adopt a new view, like this animist catfish!
Waters' alive! It's a life with it's own wish!
She shares with us all, from baptism to dog dish,
Our care cannot fall, as none can be without this.

NO PROBLEM

What trauma and turmoil has transpired today?
Our troubles and tragedies seem here to stay.

From on top of the world or from under the waves,
from our first crying breath, 'til we're put in our graves.

It seems all humankind is attracted to this.
But there are, just a few, who still achieve bliss.

You can see it said here in two million new ways.
How to love one another and each one of our days.

There's a great many issues with which we've been cursed
but, before we can help, we need to know ourselves first.

I make it sound easy, it can be quite a mean chore,
to know your own self is the only key to that door.

For me, I have Nature and there are no more tears.
My days of torture have been behind me for years.

An outcast, an alien, or a reclusive fish nut,
I know what I propose resounds in your gut.

If your saying to yourself, "this catfish ain't real",
you're denying yourself of the way that you feel.

Read what I'm saying and I think you will see,
Forget that I'm playing, it's the way it should be.

Most friends who have been around awhile now,
are used to these words, it's just my why and how.

PREDICTIONS AND PREMONITIONS

Sometimes when things go like they do
it raises the question of who's leading who.

Time and again this has been true.
Look now at this catfish who swims' leading you.

How some of us notice when something works out.
Though thoughts at first, had been fraught with doubt.

Prepare for the chance that things do work out.
To diligent awareness, I must give a shout.

There too, are times when strange forces play
revealing the sequence of some previous day.

They may take our work and the hours we'd stay
and drive us berserk or despite us, work anyway.

These odd situations where some would call luck,
fate, magic or voodoo and some other terms struck.

That's not how this fish swims and not how I truck.
I think life loves us back...unless we just suck.

WORDSWORDSWORDSWORD.
MY WEAPON OF CHOICE

Tempo and spelling are more than just telling when trying to work out a rhyme.
I throw my pen 'cross the room while screaming and yelling when the words won't work with the time.

Syntax and grammar, come down like a hammer but they're an integral part of solution.
I reconfigure my brain like some sort of programmer for word wrangling in circumlocution.

Sprites and gnomes and faeries and elves are great terms when one needs a filler
but the best words to use will come from ourselves and these are what make my rhymes killer!

All of this jargon can be a little too far gone for a white and black, fun-loving catfish,
who just wants to swim 'long with Tuna and Tarpon or float on my back and SpLaSh! Splish!

I know there are those who think to write prose is out of their realm altogether
but, if you start at the end, it's easier, my friend, as two months ago I'd written, never!

JUMPING AMBERJACKS

Fibberdegibbitts and son of a gun! This is insane! I can't believe what I've done!
A few simple words to tribute a friend and now I can't see where my fish notifs end!

To my fish foaming, your response is immense. Some of the comments have been quite intense.
Now I'm swelling with joy but, there's no suspense, as I fear once again, here with fish flatulence.

Sadly, no way, I can write for you all but, to the sea bottom, I'll not let any fall.
I have an idea. I'll post to my wall! Then I can give all a proper name call!

Now swim your sweet swim in this river called Tsu. Do all the beautiful things that you do.
Know that though absent, I still swim under you, and don't be too frightened when I surface to chew.

THE PROBLEM WITH BEING PAID TO POST

I share with you now, a tale of engagement.
An odd, askew view of what the Tsu sage meant.
"If your content is new
we'll gladly pay you".
But this maybe cause for estrangement.

What are your motives? Is, "what's in it for me?",
the reason you're here? I'd suggest that you flee.
Here, we've no taste
and think it's a waste
and are here to be real, not for money!

I enjoy this new source of friendships, of course,
but, if you can't see past greed to look,
then I highly doubt
you'll stay about
and should probably go back to Facebook.

ONE FOR THE MONEY...

One for the money is an awfully sad toad.
One not original should just hit the road.

One not for all and just here for greed
is one who'll be lost. We're a new, different breed.

One who goes marketing some popular potential
and charges for sharing, is inconsequential.

What I've seen disturbs me and it's not over yet.
This corruption needs curbing or worse, it will get.

The ones who made Tsu the platform it is,
need address this sad mess or we will lose fizz.

Each here, contributes a part of themselves.
Selling shares to new recruits is despicable and smells.

I'm just a small Tsu fish, trying to swim 'long
in a wave devoid of selfishness, we all know is wrong.

"SNORT"

Some of you know, I can be a real "sucker", with such fishy words, an ichthyologist would pucker.
I rhyme about friends I've made here on Tsu and here I have one, for another of you.

I've roasted a few with my posted review of their qualities, content and shares,
but, this fine young lady has a remarkably shady, hysterical comment for wares.

If she is amused by some content you've used, you'll know by her one word retort.
This Tsu swimming sport will write her report using no other word but a "snort"!

AN ADDRESS TO A WORD WAR MESS

Woke up, again!...but my heads all a rattle...
...some crazy dream about a poetry battle.

It was late in my day but, I circled and thrashed.
I had an advantage, a few rhymes I had stashed.

My opponent was worthy and when she cut loose
with a powerful volley, she kicked my caboose.

She rendered this catfish verbose and too lush
and with her sliver tongued savvy, proceeded to crush
this articulate fish to sniveling sea mush!
She had what it takes but, I knew this much...

With tempo so right, her cadence so sweet
I had to submit and start my retreat.
With the words she had written, this catfish was smitten
and had to run using fins just like feet!

My hopes for survival were hinged on my rival
being able to catch and release.
I was not too worried, her favor, I curried,
She wouldn't put this fish in hot grease

This is not the end, we'll both spar again,
I know that we both had some fun.
It's impossible not to with this friend I got to
and the war of rhyming words that she won.

SNOWFIRE

On out to the woodshed, I again, went last night.
The wind howled 'round, nose and ears took a bite.
Filling my wheelbarrow to fuel fires' light.
And also to keep indoor temperature right.

My trips to the woodshed are commonly when,
I'll often give pause, just to take it all in.
While I gather a load for the firewood bin
under winters' night sky and bitter cold wind.

To many, an ode to fire and cold, may seem an odd sort of
thing.
But, my trips in each night are such a delight, I'm impervious
to winter winds sting.

On out, I go, in ten feet of snow, arctic wind howling my
name.
Beckoning me to come play and be, out where most others
believe I'm insane.

MORE THAN FEISTY, THIS FISH DOTH FROTH

Shut the hell up! We don't want to hear it!
You're the damn fool that got you too near it!
Played with the flame and got yourself burned.
This searing problem, you, yourself earned.

Now stop your complaining, you're wrecking my day.
Just keep your mind shut but, get out of the way.
You may have once had the best of intentions
but, what's with the hate and your killing inventions?!?!

I won't lie to you or anyone else.
There was a time I was like yourself.
I was once fearful. I once had dread.
I too drank the poisons that made others dead!

A pampered consumer. I was one of the sheep.
Hook, line and sinker. I bit into it deep.
A captain of industry. A big C.E.O.!
I had so much nothing...and it started to grow...

I cannot tell you to what words you should listen.
I will not remind to heed intuition.
The Earth that we love, eat, breathe, drink and kiss
is turning to mud but, it used to be bliss.

SHH! QUIET! HERE THEY COME...

My woods have become more like family than most.
How I got here could be it's very own post.
This time I'll share of my life in this forest.
A tree climbing, flute playing, naked, nemophilist.

My house is quite lovely but, I prefer to be out.
Even in winter, when I snowshoe about.
Cross country skiing or out on the ice
or down on the river, under cedars so nice.

There's a seat by the water where I like to think
about Nature and life, right next to the drink.
If I stay quiet not making a sound,
some curious creatures will come gather around.

FISHY BUBBLES AND NIBBLES

I start this off without any which way, I just started writing
what my mind and heart say.
I do pick a theme
then swim consciousness stream,
so here's one for Valentines Day!

I'm not really the kind who would care. We throw words of
love everywhere.
But if you stay true
to those near to you
then any expression is fair.

You can tell I'm not the holiday type. I think each day
should get it's own hype.
But this day of love
is all I can think of
because chocolate and strawberries are ripe! Happy V-Day!
Wag n' wink! >-=^;>

NICE TO SEE THE SUN

Negative thirty on the centigrade side.
Not quite as low as I've seen it slide.
No doubt it's quite nippy and if there's any wind
this catfish will have to stay in.

From in, looking out, each window, a postcard
My fast flowing river now frozen up so hard.
Save a few places where the current obsessed,
they too, will vanish if this cold doesn't rest.

Because it's so cloudless, it's ever so bright.
Blinding white snow reflecting the sunlight.
It's the worst of the cold before winter ends.
Spring better hurry and get here, my friends.

A degree deficit has now been sold.
My time in the darkness has grown way too old.
The daylight much longer but, no warmth to behold.
For frozen fish bricks!! It's s-still r-r-really c-c-c-cold!

CATFISH WAILS OF WINTER TALES

A bite premature. A nibble bit early.
Winters this cold make a catfish get squirrely.
I need a respite, a figurative "surface for air".
I just can't seem to break free of this ice everywhere.

A SpLaT! with my tail. A nudge with my nose.
Probing each pinhole just to see if it goes.
A tropical swim could fulfill my wish.
I fear ice will overcome and I'll be more frozen fish.

And then I spot hope! A possibility comes to view!
It's in our last trying gasp, that they usually come through.
A bubbling effervescence emitting from all around.
Breath fresh with iridescence in the new friendships I've found.

NO ANIMALS WERE HURT

Some lines are so easy, they fall from my face.
And several of this one saw my fireplace.

What causes this catfish to do it?
Take a nice thought and construe it?
Like, "a lovely encounter with seahorse and flounder",
I skew into, "a splake played a fluke and he blew it".

SQIUDS

I know very little about raising a kid.
Many folks do. I never did.
An uncle thrice over, I know of the joy.
The honor, the duty, the work they employ.

My way is "old fashioned", perhaps sort of dim.
More of an attitude of, they'll sink or swim.
But, that's just my way of trying to be,
just some kind of reference for them to see.

A teacher, I'm NOT! That's a paramount lot!
That implies much more than I've got.
I'm more simple direction, some fun and affection
and a predilection for natural affection.

This fish has now spoken of the kids he's awoken, out now
swimming with you.
Go forth you guppies
you're now your own puppies,
just remember your catfish loves you.

DEDICATED TO YOU WHO GET UP AND DO

It's so hard to know what to do. And hard to know how to
be so.
It's so hard to see
who we're supposed to be
when we don't even know where to go.

I'd like to help you, I would. But I don't even think that I
could.
I'm so busy you see,
just trying to be me
I probably would not do you good.

I think I know how you feel. So I'm willing to make you
a deal.
Don't ask for help
if you won't help yourself.
We already know of that spiel.

I close this human luminosity of illogical catfish verbosity.
All I'm doing here
is a little fun with fear
But that doesn't mean it's not an atrocity.

I COULD TAKE THIS PERSONALLY

Went for my morning walk
Had my usual morning talk
with mother Nature and father time.
Together we worked out this rhyme.

With my paper in hand
Across the snow covered land.
To usual river and usual flow
but, in the days wind an oddness did blow.

For time, it was at night,
For Nature, the night, just right.
For me, an upending fright!
I tried comprehending with all my might.

Something so wrong in the night.
I spy this sadly concerning sight.
From my akimbo stance, adjusting my glance
A branch took the outhouse outright!!!

I LOVES ME SOME WORD

I find little use for being obtuse. I like to get straight to the point.
I've noticed a few,
around in this Tsu
trying to make cents in this joint.

That's okay for you, it's not what I'd do but, to each, their own in their way.
Myself, I'll astutely
pen words acutely
and adroitly circumlocute all day.

Of my words, do not fear. All I'm doing here is suggesting a way to have fun.
Some troubles so serious
it makes one delirious
So I promote this escape for everyone.

All words are divine, throw me any line. I say "bait me" with better or worse.
I think you'll enjoy it
once you employ it
and you might just write up your own verse!

FOR A TERMINALLY ILL LITTLE BOY

Hello there Bubby! I've something for you!
You may not yet know me, I am sort of new.
I've a story to tell you that's entirely true.
I think you're heroic for what you've been through!

I'm a fish that loves you! You dear little boy!
Your bright shining smile like little lit bits of joy!
This catfish now speaks of the love we employ.
And of the sea when we meet with a wet "Fish Ahoy!"

Now, on with your day. I'll be on my way,
to wait in the waves for our time to play.
Without looking ahead, make each moment stay.
Your wave riding catfish will be there that day.

NICE TO WAKE UP

Thanks everyone! For including me too!
Delighted to be here, swimming in Tsu.
Of all the fine fish, I follow a few,
some even though I'm not friends with you.

Really quite fun and you all seem so dear.
But if you might listen, I think you will hear
my comments are wordy, and my quotas aren't near.
You'll not make much money but, I am sincere.

Original content! Now I'd drink to that!
I think I have my rhyming down pat.
My pics and my words are from my own vat
of living in Nature, 'cause that's where I'm at.

THEM

Everyone's seen them. we all know they're there.
Lately it seems that they're most everywhere.
They hug then deflect you
reach out then reject you.
You sometimes can't tell if they care.

When someone lives right, it's like they're dancing on air.
Then some not so bright. It's consumer beware.
Sometimes they're heroes
and some are just zeroes
and to rhyme of these people woes, I dare.

Everyone of us faces joy and despair.
And each will decide if they spoil or spare.
Within us we share
both, biased and fair,
The question is, which will you wear?

THE THINGS WE DO FOR/TO FRIENDS

A very odd post. A most peculiar request.
It seems some wish to see a fish in a dress.
I rebuked, I denied, I refused quite flat out.
You'll not see this fish with a dress all about!

And then to add offal to suffering and injury
another flounder begs, "put the fish in a mankini!"
I had to cry out to these fish baiting squidwits,
"For fryin' up cod, even catfish have limits!"

But wait! Another yet, advised our dear Fred
as to kilts and blue paint, (this was good!), but, not on his head.
"Then add a hazard, an explosive blue thunder!"
"til the gas from his ass, (gasp!), passes best cast eyes asunder"!

A fish in a "mankini" and farting kilt with blue paint.
Or a flatfish in a black dress and "pooting" Scot with painted taint.
Thus, I've honored friends, although so cruel to do.
Now what about poor Fred? What are you going to do?...:::***>-=^;> Got blue?

A N-N-NOTHER B-B-BEAUTIFUL D-D-DAY

The propane ran out! Warm it is not! Four weeks of firewood
I've got!
I just could not write
any more rhymes last night
swimming like mad keeping fireplace hot!

My heat fuels consumption, I do closely gauge, especially
when winters like this one doth rage.
But the lid was froze down
where the needle goes around
N-N-Now my p-p-pen sh-sh-shivers off of th-th-this
p-p-page!

At thirty below when that wind starts to blow a-howling
and stacking up snow.
Even the mice
are now thinking twice
about a warmer location to go!

I must now close. My ink pen has froze and icicles hang
from my nose.
I don't mean to complain but,
C'mon propane truck!
Before supposed prose pros' toes goes

FISH BITS

At first it's awake and then it's aware.
You could add consciousness in there, somewhere.
I may be at sea or asleep at the wheel
but, I have to write to express how I feel.

I wonder, sometimes, how things might have been
if certain choices were to be chosen again.
It's not a regret that flows from this pen,
just an instant to analyse this new world we're in.

We plan for the future and learn from our past.
We know we need something if we plan to last.
Something needs doing and it needs doing fast.
Our natural resources are no longer vast!

Before our desires had led to corrupt,
Nature provided the feast for our sup.
We're now trading these meals for a poisonous cup.
I'll just write while I wait...for us all to wake up...

AROUND HERE

There's a distinct difference between there and here.
No friends or family. There are no humans here.
For my time in your cities, I did not care.
I much prefer spending time alone in solitaire.

Around here, life is real, just Nature and Earth.
These are my family, my drama and mirth.
Around here is not lonely, I'm never alone.
The trees always speaking, the drone of each stone.

Around here there's no fashion. Nothing cares about hair.
Around here I wear mukluks, waders, flannel or bare.
Around here I'm aware of each moment I live.
Around here we respect what our Mother doth give.

Around here there are times when I still fail to see
the love that my forest freely extends me.
Around here I'm a rock an animal or tree.
Around here I'm accepted for whatever I'll be.

I'LL NEVER FORGET

The smile of a child can do many things.
Remind us of youth and the wonder life brings.
The light in their eyes
at a simple surprise
and the lullaby's to them we sing.

So easy to smile at a cherubic face
even with chocolate all over the place.
A bath in the sink,
that impish wink
and dressing becomes a foot race!

So easy to envy how ready to grin. So sad to recall how we
once had been.
For we too, paraded
before we were jaded.
But, we can still share the magic they're in!

CAPTION THIS

Sifting through photos and found one quite old.
A man on a seat. His commitment was sold.
His indignation could be well foretold.
An imagination will tell of what else he did scold.

Forced consternation on his face, we behold!
Intense contamination the aforementioned then blowed.
A caption nomination for this post to unfold!?
Is there a friend in Tsu nation who could be so bold?

Anybody? No one? A phrase to uphold?
Somebody? Anyone, got any gold?
Here's what I've got, though winters now old.
It's not too fine but, at least the seat isn't cold.

NO GRAVITY. NO WEIGHT. NO ICE. JUST NICE.

I hope half the things that I've said have made their way to your head.
What I've already told you
in my attempts to unfold you
is to find out if you can be read.

It seems you prefer something light. So morbidly, I do sometimes write.
But, in this one I'll do
just a fish dance for you
that was so right in last nights moonlight.

A swim swim or SpLaSh! Some happy tailSpLaTs! Are markers to the rivers I've made.
Bubbles and nibbles
a few scrawls, I scribbles
means my dribbles have now been well laid.

I shark here and there to carp up a share, darting about everywhere.
And if in your river, I find
some bait for my mind
I'll hook on and be out of there!

FOR THE LOVE OF WINTER

The snow and the ice, although they look nice are becoming
a pain in the rear.
I really like winter
but, here in the hinter
getting iced in is something to fear.

Don't get me wrong, I love winters song, but, this one has
been way too long.
Firewood won't last,
used propane too fast
and it still seems to be coming on strong!

Still so much to do but I'm thinking of you. Just a quickie
before I depart.
To rooftop detection
then driveway inspection
and written inflection of springtime to start.

NO PICTURE REQUIRED

War. There never has been a word more profane.
Ridiculously senseless! It drives me insane!
There's no justification, no thing to explain.
How we can kill family, it's just plain inane.

Argue. Debate. Agree to be separate.
I'm going to get hostile this gets so desperate !
Don't care if you share. I know it's not pretty.
This kind of despair forgoes flowery and witty.

The squidwits in charge of the carnage that's here
perpetuate lies to lessen their fear
and to keep what they have of their worthlessness near
and whats left of the power they believe is so dear.

Use your damn drones to shoot at disease!
Or send water and food or meds if you please!

Let's bomb with hospitals! Let's bomb with schools!
But, let's stop these damn wars before we're all just dead
fools.

A RECLUSIVE CATFISH EXCURSION

I think it quite odd! I'll tell you why. I've never been social,
not even as fry.
If in December you said
these rhymes would get read
I would have told you you're high!

But as my rhyming unfolds, this catfish who holds,
anonymity oh so dear.
I'm starting to like you.
Yep, strange for me too.
Considering why I came here.

A swelling awareness! An opening of mind! A deliberate
SpLaSh! from my fishy behind!
So strange for this fish,
I kindly remind, this
social thing's new for me and you all seem so kind!

MAINTAINING A PRESENCE

There's a new definition required. A new kind of love has transpired.
We once had befriended
only those who attended.
But now amended for those who are wired.

To my new friends I now raise a toast. From inland and to each of the coasts.
From Tokyo to Peru
great getting to know you!
And love all your original posts!

But, there's a thing I'm unable to do. A few others may suffer this too.
I'm still on the fence
as to friend maintenance
I can only write and post or share things from you!

SHOCKING

Oh boy! Oh Brother! Wow, am I late! Slept in pretty good, yep it was great!

Another swell morning!

Readers, take warning!

I'm swimmingly forming some rhyme to orate!

ALMOST HAD ENOUGH WINTER

Those of us here who've seen many a winter
can recognize signs of it starting to splinter.
Now windless and sunny
it may sound funny
but, I'm a squinter in winter in the hinter!

From morning 'til nigh it's a bright sunny day! The blue sky,
a smile as if to say;
"It's still cold, and how
but, not to long now
Spring will stay and chase winter away!"

Though come along words won't bring the songbirds and
there's still so much melting of snow.
Today, it did not blow.
Quite sunny but, we know,
Winter can be so slow to go-go!

ONE MORE OF GRAVITY THEN
I NEED SWEET LEVITY

Oh for fryin' up cod! They're cutting again!
This is the worst I've seen that it's been!
And all I can do is to take up this pen!
Please tell me when this wasteful madness will end.

Do not cut them, if you please!
These are needed forest trees!
Not for building or industries
but for all us living things

Please! Let them stand! Oh Please let them be!
Please let them clear the air we all breathe!
Let them provide homes for the bird and the bee
and peace for weary minds who weep when they see...

I HAVE TO ROLL THIS SNOW
BOY ON OUT TO PLAY!

A depressive state I got myself in thinking about all the rivers I've finned.
All you fish know
we've got lots of woe
but, I got myself in a spin.

I need a bouncy little ditty! A nice light hearted one! With a swish and a tailSpLaT! and some swim, swam and swum!
There'll be time tomorrow
to rhyme about sorrow.
For this one I want to have fun!

A catfish that flashes with a tailSpLaT! that SpLaShEs!
and crashes through masses of seaweed and grasses
and passes off batches of blasphemous stashes
that matches the patches of thoughts that he hatches! Swim.. swim..SpLaSh! and grin! *>-=^;>

I CAN'T BELIEVE I DON'T HAVE AN OWL PIC!

Have you heard about the park owl in Salem? When joggers
ran by she'd assail them!
One runner who, (pun intended
was just passing through
got a hoot and a swoop and she nailed him!

SUPPORT YOUR LOCAL GROWER

I see the grief and the poisonous damage
the wasted belief in adding a bandage.
Extracted from this does give an advantage.
As we face up to the fact that we've got some baggage.

I'm so objective, I have no opinion.
It's my best perspective for choices I'm given.
My current prescription for a winning position
is a coherent restriction of consumer affliction.

Stop buying corporate disinformational views.
Start trying cooperative food farmers to use.
How you sway power is your choice to choose.
This may be the hour where we all win or lose.

WORK, WORK, WORK, PLAY! YAY!

It seems every Monday, it's so busy here.
A really gotta run day to ship beads far and near.
Still, I'm thinking of you, never have fear,
your each on my mind and to me, you are dear.

A quickie. A shorty. Just letting you know.
An into town sortie with bead orders to go.
Good use of my time allowed this short show,
of a few rhyming words, although I'm so slow.

With fierce concentration, I am trying to get
to my work's termination but, I'm not there yet.
A couple more hours then I'll be all set
to make my return as your catfishy pet.

I'M ALREADY MISSING IT

Winter is done! Deceiver days too!
Soon I'll have fun in roads that are goo.
Not quite Spring yet! There's naught I can do
but write tales of weather from here for you.

When the snow melts it can't soak the ground.
The run-off will seek, 'til the river is found.
When the ice leaves the river, it does with great sound.
That's how and when I know, Spring's coming around.

The worst of its over. I'll coast through the rest.
The threat of no firewood is no longer a pest.
It's time now for "mud season" just to keep you abreast.
And I rhyme for this reason, We've started "Drip Fest"!

WHO MIGHT YOU BE?

I might have been black. I might have been red.
A stacked word attack to rhyme whats in my head.
I may have been yellow and I may have been gray.
I may turn blue before I'm through this fishy soliloquy.

You may think I'm lost, you may think I've found
some idea I've tossed to keep fish swimming around.
I may be a catfish and I may be a trout
but, I'm not what this little fishhook's about.

Just one more rhyme. A small catfish riddle.
Can we love more or waste time diddling in the middle?
Let's say I'm affluent, monetarily.
Would you see me different or could you let that be.

Let's say I'm a thief or some crazy liar.
Or let's say my belief doesn't meet your desire.
Could I be a Muslim? What would that do?
Now I'm an Animist Buddhist Catholic too!

I might be a child and might also be old.
I may have run wild and out in the cold.
I might be a man. I might not be too.
Could I be both, would that bother you?

Everyone's something the whole world around.
No one is nothing. This is none too profound.
We can't or we can. We won't or we will.
We're all different humans. Will you love us all still?

NAMAZU HAS A DATE!

From a friend and true talent, a gift's been bestowed.
A beautiful catfish from far cross the globe!
From her own hand, (or at least, so I'm told),
My friend has donated a gift to behold!

She asked for Namazu, I didn't ask why.
I never would doubt her, I would not even try.
What a glorious sweet touch she did apply.
To a most glamorous version of Namazu and I.

A tremendous fish! An excellent specimen!
With a sexy tail swish so alluringly feminine!
Her wag and her blink makes me take a back swim.
And when we wink, wink, let the fin spins begin!

JUST SICK!

I'm stiff as a stone! Fed up with this stuff! I'm way past the red zone, had more than enough!
Corporate need to earn faster
caused another disaster!
One hundred carloads of crude crap blew up!

It crashed in the forest, fire lit up the sky. Awfully damn lucky no humans were by!
So careless for our woods
when they're moving these goods
I'd like to see the bunch of them fry!

...the insurance claims will be paid...and Earth remains maimed, I'm afraid...
We'll foot the bill
for all this and still
no attempt at restitution's been made!

FINS UP AND MAW AGAPE

A swimvitation to another friends page caused introspection to this catfishy sage.
Her question had been
how to define "real friend"
A good query but, a hard one to gauge.

Definitely depending on how you define. would determine the best way for me to choose mine.
I must like mine, real
that's just how I feel
but, I've got some damn good ones online!

I think the answer she was trying to get involved the numbers acquired in your friend set.
Online, for me
that's pretty easy,
They're all friends! We just haven't met!

MARTIANS AND VENUTIANS

I've used up my round. I've got nothing new.
I have to sit down and write up a few.
I swim 'round to your rivers, circling to chew,
some kind of idea to rhyme something for you.

A Woman'[s Day rhyme! it's the first thing in mind!
Some words about curves of the sensuous kind!
Or perhaps about peace they help all men find.
Or the unselfish deeds for the one they've refined.

Even for ladies out there on your own
who may be like me and prefer life alone.
To each I salute! And contribute this drone
of how each of you make a dwelling, a home.

KNOW THYSELF

All things in moderation or excess is best?
Is it our creation. learned or reflex?
Do you dash for the lead, cutting trail for the rest?
Or bashful and need to heed cautions behest?

Are you a controller, the one in command?
Or more a supporter in a soldiering stand?
Have you a vision to help minds expand?
We're all on a mission, to make peaceful, our land.

Without a leader, there's no one to follow.
Without some soldiers, a leader is hollow.
A leader can be, sometimes, a bit shallow.
Followers not led, most often lay fallow.

A uniting force is now nearing form.
An inviting discourse is clearing the storm.
We all have a place, since the day we were born.
And we're all in a race to keep the Earth from forlorn.

Printed in the United States
By Bookmasters